My First
REFERENCE LIBRARY

INVENTING THINGS

Adapted from Michael Holt's *Inventions*

JULIE BROWN

Gareth Stevens Children's Books
MILWAUKEE

For a free color catalog describing Gareth Stevens' list of high-quality children's books, call 1-800-341-3569 (USA) or 1-800-461-9120 (Canada).

Library of Congress Cataloging-in-Publication Data
Brown, Julie
  Inventing things / by Julie Brown and Michael Holt.
    p.   cm. — (My first reference library)
  Bibliography: p.
  Includes index.
  Summary: Describes inventions that have shaped our world from ancient
times to the present.
  ISBN 0-8368-0035-4
  1. Inventions—Juvenile literature. [1. Inventions.] I. Holt, Michael. II. Title. III. Series.
T48.H27   1989
609—dc20   89-11506

North American edition first published in 1990 by
Gareth Stevens Children's Books
RiverCenter Building, Suite 201
1555 North RiverCenter Drive
Milwaukee, Wisconsin 53212, USA

Photographic credits: Aspect Picture Library, pp. 5, 20, 55 (right); Bridgeman Art Library, pp. 8, 21 (bottom), 49; Elizabeth Whiting Associates, p. 5; Tim Furniss, p. 55 (bottom); Susan Griggs/Dimitri Ilic, p. 51; Michael Holford, pp. 15, 17 (top), 21 (top), 22, 25, 33; Hulton Picture Company, p. 51; Hutchinson Library, p. 17 (bottom); Mansell Collection, p. 53 (bottom); Mary Evans Picture Library, pp. 6, 37, 38, 41, 43; NASA, pp. 56 (right), 59; Planet Earth, p. 48; Robert Harding Picture Library, pp. 44, 58; Ronan Picture Library, pp. 7, 9 (bottom), 53 (top), 56 (left); Science Museum Library, p. 28; Science Photo Library, p. 9 (top); Spectrum Colour Library, pp. 35, 50; Topham Picture Library, p. 29

Illustrated by David Holmes and Eugene Fleury

Cover illustration © 1990 Rick Karpinski: The inside of a watch. This watch brings together many separate inventions, including levers, wheels, axles, gears, winding springs, and numbers.

Series editors: Neil Champion and Rita Reitci
Research editor: Scott Enk
Educational consultant: Dr. Alistair Ross
Editorial consultant: Neil Morris
Design: Groom and Pickerill
Cover design: Kate Kriege
Picture research and art editing: Ann Usborne
Special consultant: Dr. Gwynne Vevers

Printed in the United States of America

1 2 3 4 5 6 7 8 9 96 95 94 93 92 91 90

Contents

1: WHAT ARE INVENTIONS?

Inventions in Society

The pyramid builders used a lever to lift heavy blocks. Putting a small force on one end of the lever lets you move much heavier weights than you can by muscle power alone. You can pry open cans with levers. A see-saw is a lever that makes it easy to lift up your friend. ▼

Inventions result when someone puts old things together to make something new. All the machines and gadgets in your home are inventions. We invent things because we need or want something new. An invention is often a luxury, like perfume. Sometimes inventions are made by accident. But most inventions take long, hard work.

Invention or Discovery?

Invention is not the same thing as discovery. Discoverers find things that we never noticed before. Inventors help us use things in new ways. For example, James Watt invented an engine that uses ordinary steam. How many inventions can you see around you? Did an alarm clock wake you up today? Does a furnace heat your home? Offices and schools have computers and other machines. These are all inventions.

▲ A modern kitchen like this one has many useful inventions, including gas or electric range, blender, wax paper, microwave oven, meat thermometer, telephone, electric lights, and other handy items we use every day.

The computer has changed the way people work. ▼

Inventions and the Inventor

On December 17, 1903, ▶ at Kitty Hawk, North Carolina, the Wright brothers made the first flight in their biplane, the *Flyer*.

Who Invented What?

• Thomas Alva Edison patented over 1,000 inventions, including the light bulb and the phonograph.

• Walter Hunt invented the safety pin one day in 1846 by simply twisting a piece of wire.

• The escalator was invented in 1900 by the Otis Elevator Company.

• In 1908, Ernest Swinton of Britain invented the tank. It was first used in World War I.

How Do Inventors Work?

Most inventors work alone, and the invention is usually his or her own idea. For example, Michael Faraday invented the electric motor in England. At times, however, two people will invent the same thing without

knowing it. Joseph Henry also invented the electric motor — but he was in the United States at the time. Inventors may also work in teams. Many inventors who shared their ideas created TV. Inventors learn the laws of science, and they apply these

laws to their projects. Alexander Graham Bell had to learn the laws of electricity before he could invent the telephone.

◀ On October 18, 1892, Alexander Graham Bell first used the telephone line connecting New York and Chicago.

C. S. Cockerell invented the hovercraft, which glides over water on a cushion of air that is blown down all around the craft. ▼

Inventions, Patents, and Sales

Fun and Games

• George Ferris invented the Ferris wheel in 1893.

• A man out of work invented "Monopoly" to pretend he had money.

Bicycle Facts

• The safety bicycle replaced the risky "high-wheeler" in 1887.

• Bicycles first had air-filled tires in 1888.

• Gears came in 1889.

The pennyfarthing bicycle, ▸ also called an "ordinary," was developed in 1870. It had no gears, and the front wheel was as tall as a person's shoulders!

Patenting an Invention

Patents give inventors the right to make and sell their own inventions. They also keep other people from copying the inventor's ideas. To get a patent, inventors must prove that their idea is original.

Selling an Invention

It is easy to patent an invention, but it is often hard to sell it. For example, in 1845, R. W. Thomson patented the idea of air-filled rubber tires. But it wasn't until 1888 that air-filled bicycle tires were patented by John Dunlop. In 1894, Guglielmo Marconi invented

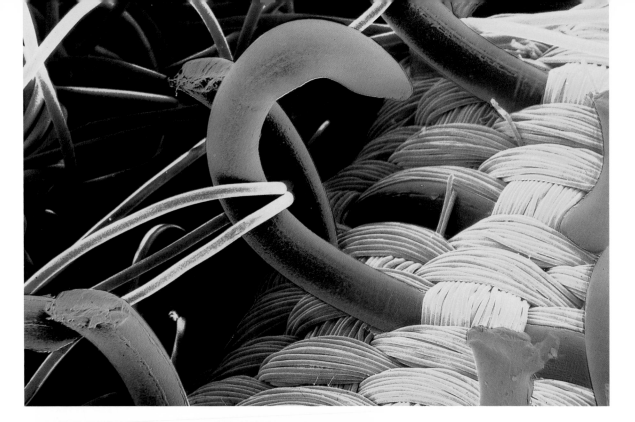

▲ The sticky burr of the burdock plant gave George de Mestral, from Switzerland, the idea for Velcro. Two pieces of Velcro cling together the same way burrs cling to animal fur — with many tiny hooks.

◀ Guglielmo Marconi (1874-1937), an Italian, developed the wireless radio. Here he is shown operating the radio on a ship at sea.

wireless telegraphy. But the idea of radio didn't catch on until the 1920s. If an inventor is lucky, many people will buy the invention. King Gillette, for instance, invented razor blades in 1895. Within ten years, he had sold 12 million blades!

2: THE EARLIEST INVENTIONS

From Making Tools to Making Money

Early Toolmaking

About 10,000 years ago, people learned how to plant and grow crops. The first farm tools were simple sticks, used to break the ground. Later, people made hoes and axes. They beat the iron out of meteorites and used the metal to make sharp blades. Hunters invented spears and the bow and arrow. People invented ways to make fire. They would hit two flint stones together to make a spark. Or they would rub sticks together until they glowed.

Cooking by Fire

People invented ways to make fire over 500,000 years ago. Soon they discovered how to cook meat. They invented cooking pots for this, probably by coating straw baskets with clay.

The Spring Trap

A small tree is tied down ▶ by a looped cord. When an animal steps into the loop, the cord is cut, and the animal is caught.

Barter and Coins

Before people invented money, they traded, or bartered, to get what they wanted. A person who had meat and needed eggs would find someone else who had eggs and needed meat. In time, people began using token goods for trading, such as beads, pots, or salt. These were easier to carry around. Later, people used gold and silver as money. The first gold coin, called the stater, was invented in Turkey 2,700 years ago. The Chinese invented the first paper money about 2,300 years ago.

▲ Stone Age people using simple inventions to hunt game, start a fire, carry water, catch fish, and make a shelter.

People once traded beads, teeth, and shells as tokens. Some Pacific islanders still use shells as tokens. ▼

From Yoke to Wheel

Did You Know?

The Egyptians floated large and heavy things on the Nile River. Levers and ramps helped them build the pyramids.

Two oxen wearing a yoke can pull a wooden plow behind them, guided by the driver. ▼

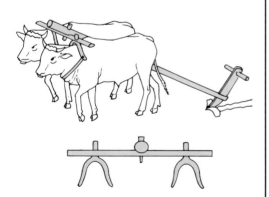

North American Indians pulled the loaded travois behind their horses. ▶

Long ago, people invented easier ways to carry large and heavy loads. Around 6000 BC, they began putting yoke and harness on cattle to pull plows. Other people put packsaddles on horses so they could carry loads. Some Siberian and North American Indians still use the travois, a carrying sling dragged behind a horse.

Using the Wheel

People may have first used the wheeled cart in Mesopotamia — now Iraq — in about 3500 BC. These carts had an axle that turned with the wheels. Someone always had to grease the axle to help it turn in its leather sling.

Sumerians invented an axle that stayed still while only the wheel turned. This was the first great mechanical invention. But the wheel had other uses. Ancient Babylonians used water wheels to irrigate their crops. Romans used wheels to grind grain.

▲ In this Mesopotamian city, oxen pull a cart. The cart's fixed axle turns along with the wheels.

Rotating axle   **Fixed axle**

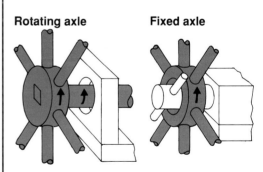

▲ This drawing shows the difference between a rotating axle and a fixed axle.

◀ This early water wheel uses animal power to bring up the water.

Words and Numbers

Writing and the alphabet

The Sumerians were the first people to develop a form of writing. They used picture symbols to stand for things, like cows or arrows. Other words could be shown by using picture symbols of things that sounded the same as the word. We still use the idea in simple rebuses where, for instance, a picture of an eye can stand for the word "I." The Egyptians and the Chinese used other picture word systems. Then came the alphabet that used signs for sounds. The Semites of Syria and Palestine, and later the Phoenicians, invented about thirty signs, each one standing for a consonant. The Greeks also used vowel signs. Then any word could be written down easily.

The invention of numbers

At about the same time as writing was developing, number systems came into use. The Babylonians, Sumerians, Mayans, Chinese, and Hindus all invented number systems. The Chinese invented the abacus, a simple counting device with sliding beads on rods. It is still used today. The greatest number invention, zero, was devised by the Hindus in about AD 600. It allowed people to write very large numbers using only ten symbols — the numbers *1* to *9*, and zero.

O + 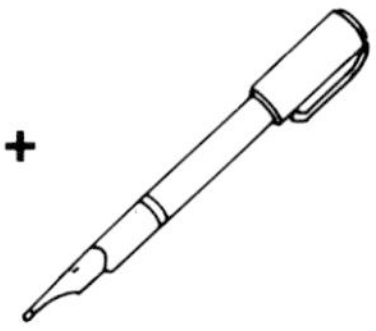

o + pen = open

P + 

p + ark = park

 **+ 4**

bee + 4 = before

▲ A simple rebus, showing how words can be made by using picture symbols.

The development of the alphabet is shown here. ▶

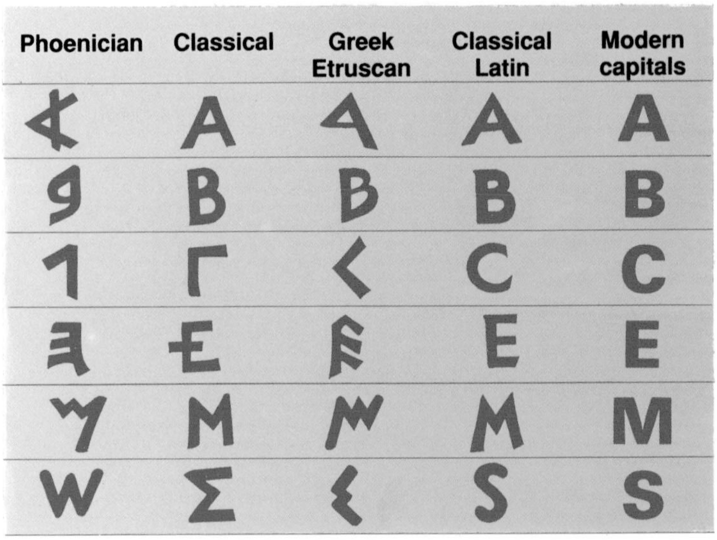
Phoenician
Classical
Greek Etruscan
Classical Latin
Modern capitals
A
B
C
E
M
S

The Rosetta Stone was discovered in 1799. It has the same message in three kinds of writing: Egyptian hieroglyphs (top), simple Egyptian writing (middle), and Greek (bottom). An understanding of Greek helped a linguist figure out the hieroglyphs.

Papermaking

Paper gets its name from papyrus, a reed the Egyptians wrote on. The Chinese made paper from tree bark.

Paper Facts

• Europeans once made paper from linen rags.

• In 1798, a new machine made paper in long pieces instead of short strips.

• Friedrich G. Keller invented a machine in 1840 to make paper from wood, as we do today.

Here is a Chinese abacus, similar to those used long ago. Each bead stands for a different number. The number arranged on this abacus is 687,235,100. The user flicks beads toward the center to make calculations. Skilled users can work faster on an abacus than others can on a calculator!

15

Ancient City Builders

Egyptian Facts

• The Egyptians invented the harp, the lyre, and other stringed musical instruments.

• The Egyptians used knotted ropes to measure triangles when building.

• They also invented the *shaduf*, which lifts water out of a river.

Both Greek and Roman city builders took the idea of the arch from the Egyptians. The Romans used the arch in a new way, for bridges. They put vaulting roofs, instead of beams, on their buildings. The Romans invented the crane for lifting heavy things. They also used the block and tackle, a system of pulleys, and they invented a special knife for surgery.

Greek Inventions

Archimedes was the greatest inventor in ancient Greece. He invented a device for lifting water that is still used along the Nile. He was also the first person to figure out how levers and pulleys worked. The Greeks

Around 250 BC, Archimedes invented the Archimedes' screw. Turning the handle brings water up through the pipe and out at the top. It both irrigated and drained land in the Nile valley.

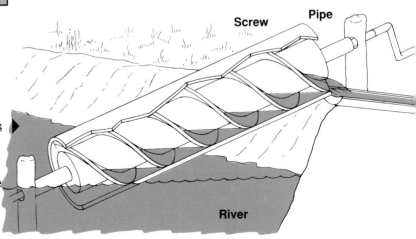

Screw **Pipe**

River

16

▲ A Roman aqueduct built
in France about 2,000 years
ago to carry water.

invented a new kind of clepsydra, which is a kind of clock that uses dripping water to tell time. The Greeks invented the ruler and compass to help in drawing. They borrowed the Egyptian idea of the right triangle to develop the mathematics of geometry.

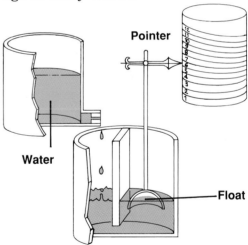

Pointer

Water

Float

▲ A Greek clepsydra, or water clock. Dripping water lifted the pointer. The line it pointed to told the time.

◀ The shaduf is a bucket on a long pole. A weight on one end helps this man lift water from the river to irrigate his field.

17

3: INVENTION ON THE MOVE

Moving People and Things

Getting around on Land

In central Asia, people invented saddles for riding horses. Then, in India, stirrups added to the saddles made horseback riding easier and safer. The horse collar, a Chinese invention of the sixth century, allowed horses to pull plows and carts. Horseshoes, invented by the Romans, helped horses walk on the stone roads.

Getting around on Water

Early towns were usually built on the banks of rivers, such as the Tigris, the Euphrates, and the Nile. People learned to cross over water by using logs as floats.

A modern blacksmith nails a horseshoe onto a horse's hoof. The nails go into the hoof's hard horn rim. This does not harm the horse in any way. ▼

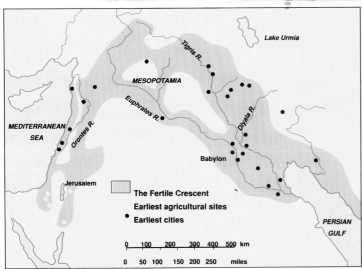

A sail helped Nile boats go much farther.

◄ A map of Mesopotamia. The name means "between the rivers" — the Tigris and Euphrates rivers.

Wind

Cloak

The First Sail?

▲ Someone wearing a cloak might have stood up in a boat. When the wind caught his or her robes, it blew the boat along the water.

The first boats were canoes made by hollowing out logs. People built the first rafts from reeds, bamboo, or wood. The Egyptians made riverboats out of reeds. To be able to fish from boats, early fishermen invented fishing nets, rods, line, and hooks.

Sailing Ships

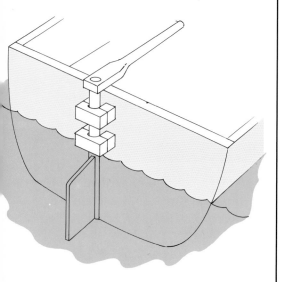

The first sailors were probably the Cretans. They sailed over the Mediterranean Sea in galleys powered by oars around 3000 BC. By 1500 BC, the Phoenicians had invented seagoing ships, called biremes, that had two levels of oars on each side. The Greeks developed a galley that moved by both oars and sails. The Greeks were excellent sailors and traveled to many distant places.

Improvements in Sailing

By AD 800, the Norsemen built their longships with sturdy keels. A sailor steered the longship by an oar attached to the starboard, or "steer board," side. Around AD 1100, the Norsemen invented the first true sternpost rudder. This made steering easier. Then

▲ When the handle of a rudder is pulled to the left, the rudder moves right. This steers the boat to the right.

Arabs have been sailing ▶ *dhows* like this for over 1,000 years.

▲ This bowl shows a Greek galley with oars, sails, and a battering ram.

◀ Norsemen sailed across the Atlantic in longships.

The world as mapmakers saw it around AD 40. ▼

sailors could sail out of sight of land. They invented ways of finding their route by using the stars as a guide. Soon people made maps of seacoasts, as well as maps of the stars. So began the science of navigation.

Finding the Way

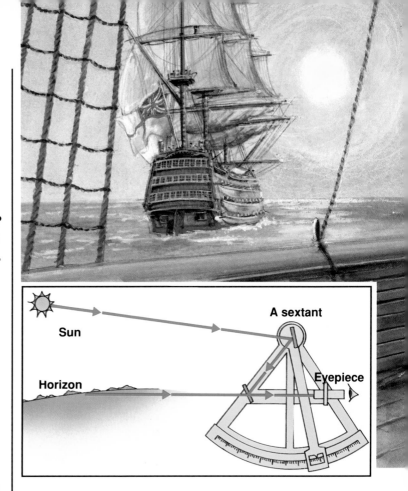

▲ This astrolabe was made in Germany in 1548 by George Hartman.

Several inventions helped sailors find their way at sea. The astrolabe, probably invented around 150 BC by the Greek Hipparchus, was pointed at a star to find its angle above the horizon. Sailors could then figure out where the ship was. The Chinese invented the compass. They used a piece of magnetic lodestone balanced on a needle so it could always point north. A compass card helped sailors read directions.

Using a Sextant

◀ A sailor sights the Sun
through the smoky glass
of the eyepiece. He or she
moves a mirror to line up
the Sun with the horizon
and then reads the angle.

Lodestone

Needle

◀ The magnetic lodestone
turns on the needle point of a
compass. You can read the
direction on the card. ▼

Later Inventions

John Hadley in England and
Thomas Godfrey in the United
States invented the sextant.
With it, sailors could sight the
stars more easily. This helped
them find the ship's exact
location north or south. Staying
on their route meant that ships
with cargo could reach their
ports at about the right time.

Compass

4: INVENTIONS FOR WAR

Slings and Catapults

▲ This Roman soldier is ready for battle. He wears a bronze helmet and, for his armor, iron bands on leather.

Fighting Facts

• The Assyrians invented the fighting tower around 900 BC.

• The Chinese invented the crossbow about 500 BC.

From early times, people have invented weapons for war. A simple one was the sling. This hurled stones farther and harder than they could be by hand. In Sumer, horse-drawn chariots carried soldiers into battle. By 1100 BC, the Persians made lighter and faster chariots with two wheels and an axle that turned. After people learned how to make bronze, they invented swords. Roman soldiers built an early battering ram — a tree trunk, tipped with metal, that swung from ropes. They also made long ladders to use in climbing up enemy city walls.

Catapults

The Greeks used a catapult that could fire stones or arrows. The Chinese designed the trebuchet, a giant slingshot that could throw missiles even farther. Europeans made one much like it, called the onager. Romans built a small catapult, powered by twisted ropes.

▲ Here is an early Persian war chariot from about 1100 BC. It had two free-turning wheels with many spokes. One warrior could drive the chariot in battle. The four horses that pulled it could gallop up to 40 miles per hour (64 kph)!

◀ This catapult is being wound up, ready for firing. By twisting the ropes, the soldiers would prepare the catapult to hurl large boulders toward enemies.

Gunpowder and Cannons

The Chinese invented gunpowder, the first human-made explosive, around the ninth century AD. They used it for fireworks and rockets. When gunpowder came to Europe in 1242, people used it to improve the methods of warfare.

Cannons on Land and Sea

On land, cannons soon replaced the catapult and the battering ram. Cannons were cheaper, and they were easier to move around. Cannonballs could smash down the walls of castles and cities. The hand-held musket is also a cannon — it shoots smaller balls. At sea, cannons replaced the older fighting methods of ramming other ships and setting them on fire. Ships with cannons could sink other ships at a distance.

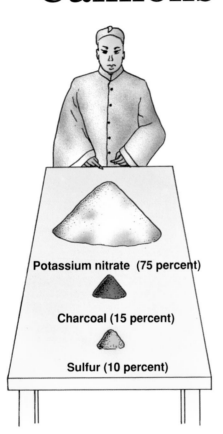

Potassium nitrate (75 percent)

Charcoal (15 percent)

Sulfur (10 percent)

▲ The Chinese mixed these ingredients to make gunpowder. When lighted with a match, the mixture explodes!

A musket is really a small cannon, held by hand. ▶

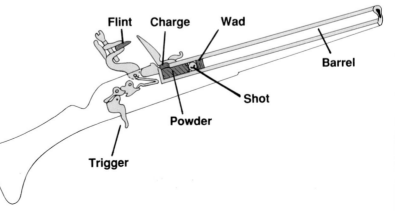

Flint   Charge   Wad

Barrel

Shot

Powder

Trigger

The "Big Bang" in Science

Gunpowder brought many important changes to science. The making of gunpowder led to the science of chemistry. The need to aim cannons led to the sciences of ballistics and gunnery. Scientists learned about heat when they made cannons. All of these changes helped bring on the Industrial Revolution.

▲ During sea battles, nearly all the guns on board fired out of the sides of the ships.

Gunners had to figure out where the cannonball would land. This led to the science of ballistics. ▼

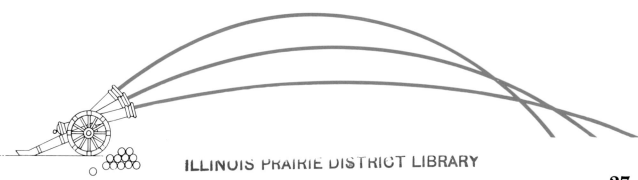

5: THE ADVANCE OF SCIENCE

Leonardo da Vinci

Leonardo da Vinci (1452-1519) was an architect, a craftsman, an artist, and an engineer. He was a great genius of the Italian Renaissance period. He filled many notebooks with his ideas and sketches. Most of his inventions were way ahead of their time and were not built.

Leonardo's Inventions

His greatest invention on paper was the flying machine. After watching the way birds flew, Leonardo made many models for machines to help humans fly. All of his plans were superbly drawn. They include these:

- An armored car driven by cranks and pedals
- An alarm clock that worked by tilting the sleeper's bed
- A diving suit that let a person stay under water for four hours

Backward Writing

Leonardo made 7,000 pages of notes. He wrote most of his notes backward and read them with a mirror.

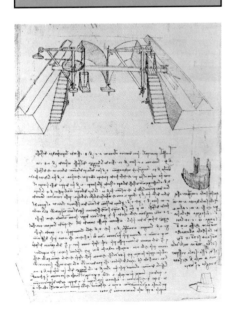

▲ This is a page from one of his notebooks showing sketches of his ideas.

Leonardo used his inventive
mind in his successful career as
a military and civil engineer.

- A submarine
- A crude kind of helicopter
- Pumps to empty water out
of mines
- Rolling mills to shape metal
into sheets

▲ In 1988, a wooden model
of a flying machine was
built based on a design by
Leonardo. It looks very
much like a bird's wings
but it would not have flown.

◀ Leonardo was a great
artist, and he influenced
painting for a hundred years
afterward. His most famous
paintings are the *Mona Lisa*
and the *Last Supper*. He was
a great scientist, too, and
studied geology, biology, and
mathematics. He also knew
how to work brass and other
kinds of metal.

From Near and Far

The Egyptians invented glass before 3000 BC. Later, the Arabs discovered how to grind glass into lenses. They learned how to focus with a magnifying glass. By 1350, many Italians wore eyeglasses, or spectacles. Around 1600, a Dutch lens grinder's assistant saw that looking through two lenses made faraway things seem much larger. In 1609, Galileo Galilei made the first known telescope used to study the stars and the planets.

▲ These spectacles were made in the early 1500s.

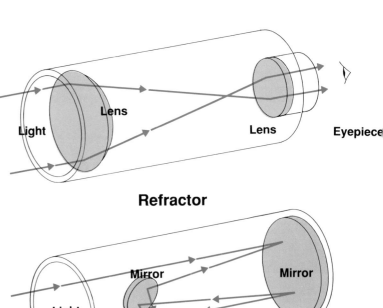

Refractor

The simple refracting ▶ telescope (upper) is called the Galilean, after the famous astronomer. The big lens magnifies the image. In the reflecting telescope (lower), a mirror magnifies the image instead of a lens.

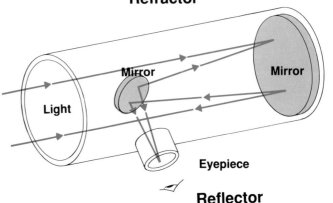

Reflector

▲ Anton van Leeuwenhoek used tiny, perfect lenses he ground himself to study stagnant water, blood, and scrapings from teeth. To make this microscope (below), he put lenses between sheets of brass. The rod held the specimen he wanted to examine.

The World of Small Things

The first microscope probably was made in 1590 by a Dutch spectacle maker. Anton van Leeuwenhoek, also Dutch, made tiny lenses that magnified things over 200 times. He saw things that no one had seen before, like bacteria and tiny water fleas living in a drop of water!

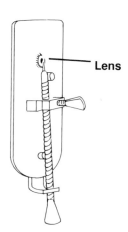

Lens

Telling Time

Galileo swings a simple pendulum. In 1657, Christiaan Huygens designed the first pendulum clock. ▼

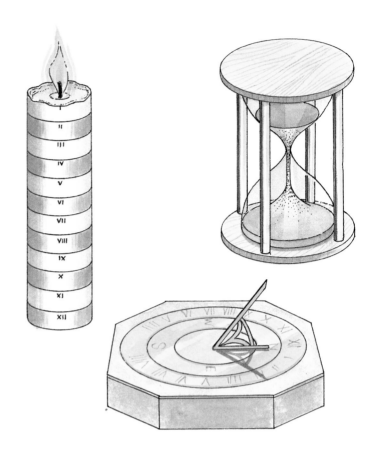

The very first clocks were sundials that told time from shadows cast by the Sun. Next came candle clocks that burned down to hour marks, water clocks that dripped, and hourglasses filled with sand. The first mechanical clocks may have been geared astrolabes used by sailors. In the late Middle Ages, the escapement was invented. This is a moving catch that controls a clock's gears. Churches used these clocks. Galileo first thought of using a pendulum in clocks.

▲ This 1386 clock in Salisbury Cathedral, England, is the world's oldest working clock.

This is the chronometer that John Harrison designed. It solved the problem of finding longitude — a ship's east-west position. ▼

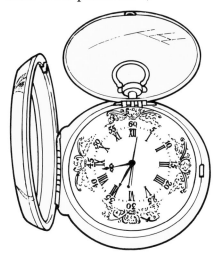

A Timepiece for Navigators

Sextants helped tell a ship's position north or south. But to figure its position east or west, navigators needed to know the exact time. Robert Hooke, of England, replaced the clock's pendulum with small wind-up gears for the first chronometer. John Harrison made the first truly accurate timepiece in 1764. It was the size of a pocket watch and kept nearly perfect time. Navigators could use it to figure their ship's position correctly.

Water Mills and Windmills

In the Middle Ages, water mills were a source of power. Mills used triphammers and cranks, both Chinese inventions. The water mill was used for grinding grain and pounding metal. Nearly every wealthy household had a water mill and a miller to operate it. Millwrights were men who traveled around the country, building and repairing mills.

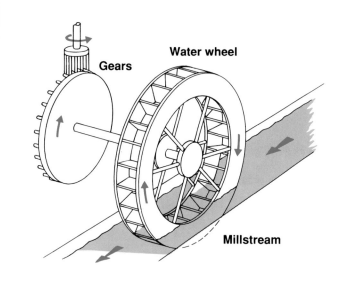

The water wheel shown here is turned by water flowing ▶ under it. The wheel turns the gears.

The typical Middle Ages ▶ manor house had a water wheel. It would turn spits for roasting and power other simple machines.

◀ Windmills like this one in Holland have four sails made of wooden slats that catch the wind. The mills once pumped water or ground grain.

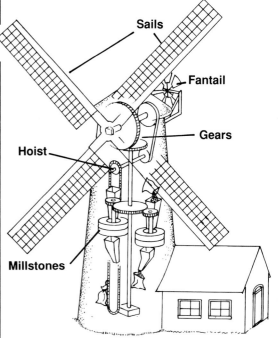

Sails

Fantail

Gears

Hoist

Millstones

▲ This sketch shows how the windmill works. A fantail turns the top of the windmill so the sails always face into the wind. The sails turn the cogs and gears that give power to the millstones.

Windmills

Windmills, like sails, harness the power of the wind. The Chinese used windmills for irrigating the land and for grinding grain. By 1150, windmills were used in France, Holland, Belgium, and Spain. Like water mills, they ground grain. Windmills were also used for washing clothes, blowing air into furnaces, and sawing wood. In the eighteenth century, windmill power was used for spinning and weaving cloth.

From Print to Air Pressure

Early Printing

The Chinese invented printing with wooden blocks about AD 770. Pi Sheng made movable type from clay in the 1040s for printing Buddhist prayers.

Printing

Around 1440, a German goldsmith, Johann Gutenberg, invented a way to print with movable metal type. He made letters that could be arranged in any way in a frame. In this way, he could make up many different pages, using the type over and over. He also invented the printing press. The first book ever printed was the Bible.

Other Inventions

Galileo invented the water thermometer. It had a bulb as big as a hen's egg and a long tube. One of his pupils invented the barometer, which measures air pressure. Later, Gabriel Daniel Fahrenheit made the mercury thermometer and scale

Here is Otto von Guericke's famous experiment. In the German emperor's park, he showed the effects of a vacuum. The air pressure outside the globe was stronger than even 16 horses!

of degrees that we still use. In 1642, Blaise Pascal invented the adding machine in France. It used gears. Otto von Guericke of Germany invented an air pump. In 1654, he pumped all the air out of two copper half globes. The air pressure outside held the halves so tightly that 16 horses couldn't pull them apart!

◀ Johann Gutenberg shows two printed pages to his friends.

▲ Barometers like this one are used to predict the weather from changes in air pressure.

6: THE INDUSTRIAL REVOLUTION

Coal Mining and Engines

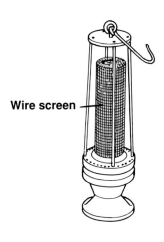

Wire screen

▲ Sir Humphry Davy's safety lamp. The wire screen kept the lamp's flame from causing gas explosions in mines.

The swift spread of machines and factories in the 1700s is called the Industrial Revolution. It gave work to the many country people who moved to the cities of Europe and North America. Wooden machines wore out, so people then made machines of iron. But iron had to be smelted with huge fires. The smelter fires burned coal that was dug out of the ground and brought by horse-drawn wagons. The coal mines had to be kept dry so the miners could work. But water kept leaking in.

Long ago, miners dug ▶ coal out by hand in mines like this. Today, they use machines.

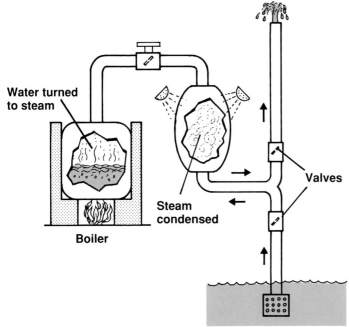

Water turned to steam

Boiler

Steam condensed

Valves

Savery's steam engine pumping water out of a mine shaft. Steam condensed in the tank, making a vacuum that sucked water up the pipe into the tank. Then more steam drove the water out of the tank and up the pipe. Valves controlled the flow of steam and water.

Mining Safety

Captain Thomas Savery of England found a way to keep the coal mines dry. In 1698, he patented a steam-driven engine that pumped water out of the mines. He called it "The Miner's Friend." Thomas Newcomen designed a better pump engine, but it burned a lot of coal. Later, James Watt would invent a much better steam engine. A big danger for miners was that the lamps they used could set off explosions of the gas in the mines, killing them. In 1815, Sir Humphry Davy invented a miner's safety lamp. Wire gauze protected the flame.

▲ A cutaway view of Thomas Newcomen's steam engine pumping water out of a mine. It used a rocking beam to work a piston inside a cylinder. Unlike Savery's engine, this one worked above the ground.

The Age of Steam

Travel Facts

• John Loudon McAdam invented an asphalt road surface, called tar macadam.

• Richard Trevithick's steam engine moved on rails, but very slowly.

• George Stephenson built a locomotive that ran up to 20 mph (32 kph)!

The Steam Engine on Land

James Watt, an instrument maker in Scotland, had an idea for improving the steam engine. Instead of having the steam heat and cool in the same cylinder, he used a second cylinder where the steam could condense back into water. Watt patented this invention, and the steam engine was born. He also patented a device called a governor that helped the engine run at an even speed. In 1801, Englishman Richard Trevithick first used a steam engine that ran a carriage slowly. George Stephenson invented the exhaust funnel so the fire burned hotter, giving the steam engine more power.

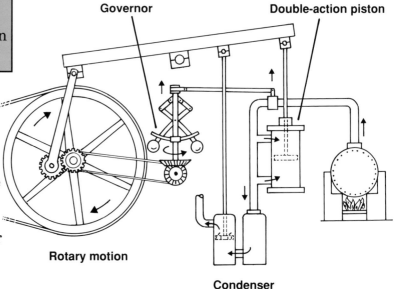

Governor

Double-action piston

Rotary motion

Condenser

James Watt's steam engine used a separate condenser for cooling steam. This allowed the heated cylinder to stay hot, so the engine worked much better.

GEO. STEPHENSON'S ROCKET, 1829.

Steamboats

Denis Papin of France invented the steam-powered paddle-wheel boat in 1707, but angry boatmen wrecked it. In the United States, Robert Fulton built the first steam-powered passenger boat in 1807 — the *Clermont*.

▲ The *Rocket* — Stephenson's most famous "Puffing Billy."

Seagoing Facts

• John Fitch first invented the passenger steamboat, in 1787, but no one cared. He died penniless.

• The *Clermont* was the first paying-passenger steamboat.

• The first steamer to cross the Atlantic was the *Savannah*. It made a record trip in 29 days.

◀ The *Clermont* — the first passenger-carrying steamship.

The Spinning Industry

The Textile Revolution

The Industrial Revolution's biggest impact was on the industry that made cloth, or textiles. In the 1700s cotton, picked by slaves, was shipped from North America and the West Indies to England. There it was made into fabric. Early spinners and weavers worked in their own homes. Later, steam-powered machines moved cloth making into textile factories.

Textile Facts

• The spinning jenny could spin 16 threads at one time, instead of only one like the old spinning wheels. The word "jenny" was a nickname for "gin" or "engine."

• The spinning frame was patented in 1769. This device used water power for spinning thread.

• Eli Whitney's cotton gin feeds cotton fiber through a row of saws. Teeth on the saws pull the cotton from the seeds.

• The spinning mule, invented in 1779, was a combination of the spinning jenny and the spinning frame. It made very fine yarn.

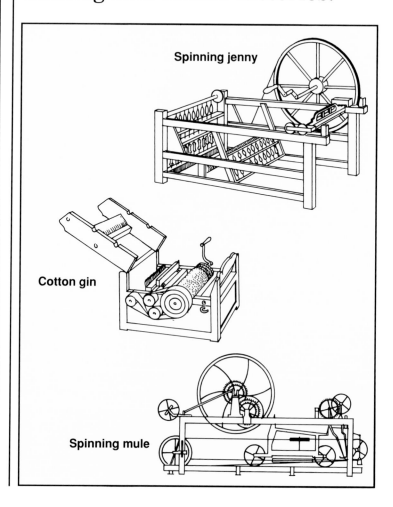

Spinning jenny

Cotton gin

Spinning mule

Speeding up Production

In 1767, the spinning jenny was invented to spin cotton swiftly into thread. Other spinners then invented included the spinning mule and the spinning frame. In 1789, Edmund Cartwright invented the power loom. In North America, Samuel Slater built the first cotton mill in 1793. Eli Whitney, also in 1793, invented the cotton gin that mechanically removed the seeds from the cotton fibers. The ring-spinning frame was invented in the United States in 1828.

▲ A nineteenth-century textile factory was a grim place. The noise was deafening and accidents were common. Women and children worked long hours, six days a week, for low wages.

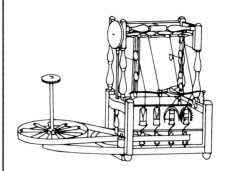

Spinning frame

The Metal Revolution

As the Industrial Revolution expanded, iron and steel were needed more and more for machines and for the factories that made machines.

Making Iron

Long ago, people made iron by putting the ore into a hot charcoal fire. They used bellows to force air into the fire to make it burn hotter. The melted iron collected in a lump. Abraham Darby burned coke, made from coal, for a hotter fire than from burning charcoal. Air blown in by Watt's steam engine produced a fire that was even hotter.

The Secret of Steel Making

Steel had been made for 4,000 years. But in 1722, Frenchman Rene de Réaumur found that

This steel-making furnace ▶ is loaded with scrap steel, iron ore, and limestone. When these are heated, pig iron is added. Molten steel is then taken out.

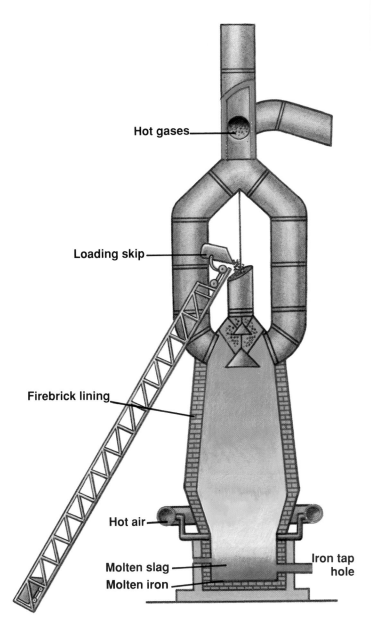

Hot gases

Loading skip

Firebrick lining

Hot air

Molten slag

Molten iron

Iron tap hole

◀ Iron is made in a blast furnace like this. The furnace is lined with brick and cooled with water. Molten iron is taken out every few hours. Some furnaces make 3,000 tons per day!

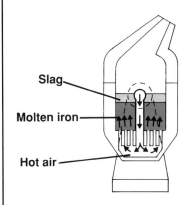

Slag

Molten iron

Hot air

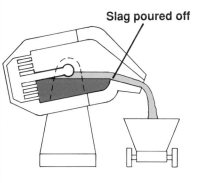

Slag poured off

adding the right amount of carbon to steel made it hard and springy for tools and machines. Gilchrist Thomas invented a steel furnace that was lined with limestone so it could use impure iron. Steel production soared.

▲ Henry Bessemer invented the Bessemer converter for making steel. It can tip to the side for adding limestone. Then it tips upright, and air blows into it from below to burn out the impurities.

The Age of Electricity

Static Electricity

In 1745, a German clergyman named E. J. von Kleist made a device called a Leyden jar that could store static electricity. Benjamin Franklin later showed that lightning was the same force as the spark in the jar, but much more powerful.

Current Electricity

In 1800, Alessandro Volta invented a battery that stored current electricity. Michael Faraday discovered he could

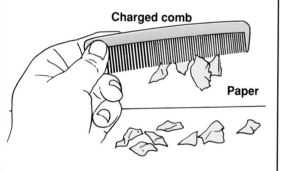

▲ Static electricity, created by rubbing a comb through your hair, can pick up small bits of paper with its positive charge.

Volta's battery was ▶ made up of round disks of copper, zinc, and cloth soaked in acid. With more disks added, Volta could make more powerful sparks.

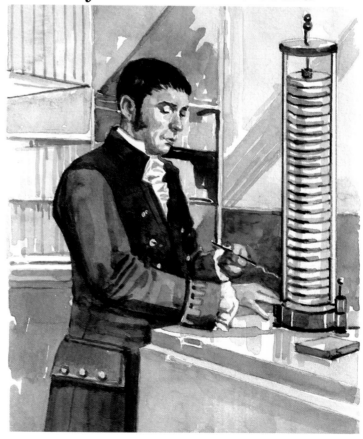

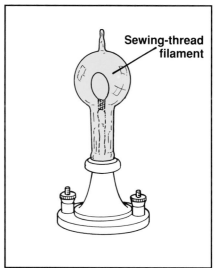

◀ Michael Faraday invented the electric generator and the electric motor. Here he shows how magnets can generate electricity.

Sewing-thread filament

generate current electricity by moving a magnet inside a wire coil. This led to large machines generating electricity. By the 1890s, electricity was being used to light whole cities. Faraday also invented electroplating — depositing a thin layer of metal over an object. In 1895, Wilhelm Röntgen, a German, invented the x-ray tube.

▲ Thomas Alva Edison, a great US inventor, made the first workable light bulb in 1879. He used a cotton thread in a glass bulb.

Farming and Food

Food Facts

• In 1831, Cyrus Hall McCormick invented the reaper for cutting wheat.

• McCormick's factory in Chicago sold 4,000 farm machines a year.

• Hippolyte Mege Mouries of France invented margarine, which means "pearly."

• In 1939, Franklin Kidd patented a fast method of freeze-drying food.

This powerful modern tractor is pulling a disk plow. The cabin keeps the farmer from being crushed if the tractor tips over. This tractor has wheels, but others have continuous tracks. ▶

Growing Food

As more people moved to cities, more cheap food was needed to feed them. Farmers began to raise big food crops to sell for money. Several inventions helped increase production. In England, farmers began using drill plows and horse harrows. In the United States, farmers used the newly invented tractor and combine harvester.

Cooking and Preserving

Denis Papin of France made the first pressure cooker. It could

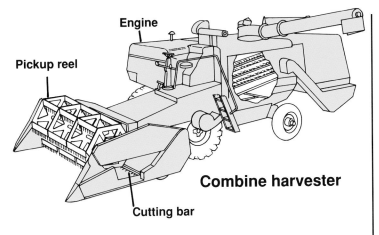

Engine

Pickup reel

Combine harvester

Cutting bar

◀ The combine harvester is both a reaper and a thresher. It was widely used in the wheat plains of North America after 1917. Today, most farming countries use combine harvesters.

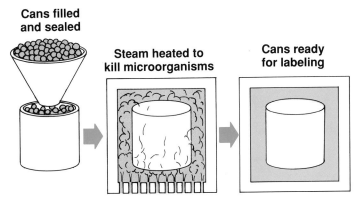

Cans filled and sealed

Steam heated to kill microorganisms

Cans ready for labeling

◀ Canning is one way of preserving food so it will not spoil. Fruit, meat, and vegetables are canned in very clean factories. Food can stay fresh for a year or more in cans. Englishman Peter Durand first put food in cans in the 1800s.

cook foods hotter and faster. Nicholas Appert, also French, invented the process of bottling fruit that led to canned foods. Today we add chemicals to some foods to keep them from spoiling. We often wrap food in cellophane, invented in the early 1900s by Jacques Brandenburger. The first quick-frozen food came in the 1920s. Around 1770, Joseph Priestley added a gas, carbon dioxide, to water, hoping it would cure the disease of scurvy. But instead, he invented soda water.

▲ Joseph Priestley (1733-1804) was a British chemist.

49

Oil and Gas

Opposite, right: This ▶▶ drilling platform in the North Sea drills into the seabed to reach the gas underneath the rock.

Oil Facts

• In 1859, Edwin Drake struck oil in Pennsylvania.

• Britain's James Young found a way to get kerosene from shale, a kind of rock.

• Abraham Gesner, of Canada, boiled crude oil to get kerosene from it.

Gasoline, diesel oil, and ▶ other products come from oil refineries like the one shown here.

The Oil Industry

People have used petroleum since ancient times. In the Bible Noah waterproofed his ark with petroleum. The Egyptians used petroleum to grease chariot axles. Inventions for getting kerosene from shale and oil came in the 1850s. Kerosene was burned in lamps and stoves. Edwin L. Drake started the oil industry when he drilled the first deep oil well in 1859. Samuel van Syckel built the first oil pipeline. Today, oil travels through pipes for thousands of miles.

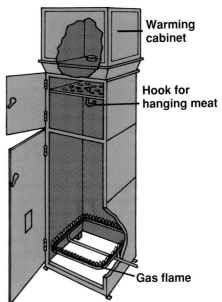

Warming cabinet

Hook for hanging meat

Gas flame

▲ Homes in the 1800s used gas ovens like this one.

The Gas Industry

In 1792, William Murdock invented gas lighting to replace candles. By 1850, many towns in Europe and North America were using gas to light their streets and houses. In 1832, James Sharp invented gas stoves for cooking. Soon gas stoves were in use throughout the United States and Britain. Most gas used today is natural gas, from wells in the North Sea and the United States.

Gas Facts

• In 1780 Antoine Lavoisier invented a gas-holding storage tank.

• Frederick Albert Winsor, of Germany, formed the world's first gas company in 1813.

• In 1885, Carl Auer invented the gas mantle, a fine mesh placed over a flame to give off light.

• Robert Bunsen invented the gas Bunsen burner that is widely used in laboratories.

7: | 20TH-CENTURY TECHNOLOGY

Mass Production

These finished cars are rolling off the final assembly line at the Ford Motor Company in Detroit. The car body slid down a ramp and landed on its wheels! ▼

Mass production has greatly changed the way people make things. After the American Revolution (1775-1783), Eli Whitney invented a way to make guns, using the same standard-size parts. This was an early step toward mass production. Later, Samuel Colt used Whitney's mass production ideas in his own factory when he manufactured the gun he had invented, the Colt revolver.

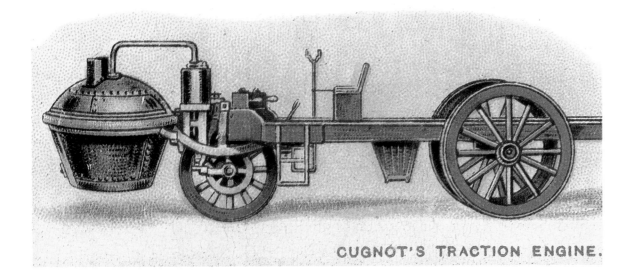
CUGNOT'S TRACTION ENGINE.

The Automobile

In 1769, Nicolas Cugnot made the first successful steam-driven car. In the late 1800s, electric cars became popular after Camille Faure invented a car battery to store electricity. The first car to run on gasoline was built by Etienne Lenoir in 1860. Ransom E. Olds built cars by using an assembly line, but it was Henry Ford who perfected this method of manufacturing. In Detroit, Ford built his famous Model T Ford, which was very cheap for its day. In this way the modern automobile industry began. Today, auto factories use computer-controlled robots to do the work that humans once did.

▲ Nicolas Cugnot's steam traction engine, built in the 1760s, was the first true automobile. It had a single front wheel. In front of it hung the boiler and engine. Cugnot, a French army officer, made this tractor to pull a cannon.

▲ Karl Benz, the first man to build a gasoline-driven car for sale to the public.

Flight

The Montgolfier brothers' balloon

Here are three kinds of ▶ flying machines: a hot-air balloon (left), a biplane (middle), and an airship (right). The balloon was flown in front of King Louis XVI of France in 1783. Early biplanes had fixed wheels for landing. *La France* could travel at the speed of 14 mph (23 kph)!

People have always dreamed of flying. The first flight was made by the Montgolfier brothers in a balloon in 1783. In 1804, Sir George Cayley invented a glider. *La France* was the name of the first steam-powered airship, built in 1884. The Wright Brothers built the first powered heavier-than-air machine in 1903. They had to invent all the parts themselves, including the engine. In the 1920s, people began making airplanes out of metal instead of fabric and wood. Early airplanes were biplanes, with two sets of wings.

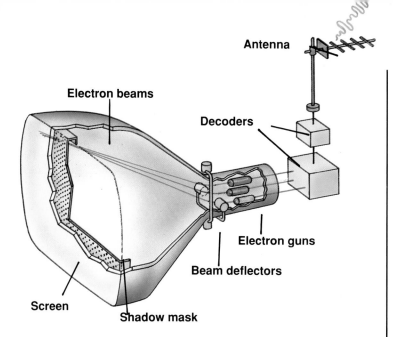

Antenna

Electron beams

Decoders

Electron guns

Beam deflectors

Screen

Shadow mask

◀ The television antenna picks up signals from the television station. These are decoded and shot onto the screen. The shadow mask guides the beams to strike dots on the screen that are colored red, green, and blue.

Television

The Crookes tube, which gave off light when hit by electrons, and the photoelectric cell, which turned light into electricity, both made television possible. After 1945, TV spread widely. Color TV began in the US in 1953. The first satellite TV message was sent in 1962. A 1965 US space probe sent television pictures of Mars' surface to Earth.

Communications Facts

• The first words Bell spoke into his telephone were: "Mr. Watson, come here! I want you!"

• The first words Thomas Edison recorded on his phonograph were: "Mary had a little lamb."

• Baron Jons Berzelius invented the photoelectric cell, which turned light signals into electricity.

• Philo T. Farnsworth, John Logie Baird, and Vladimir Zworykin all helped invent television.

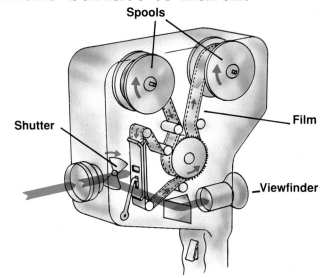

Spools

Shutter

Film

Viewfinder

◀ A movie camera takes pictures the same way a regular camera does. The film is divided into frames, though, and the camera stops for a split second for each frame that is shot.

Computers
and
the Future

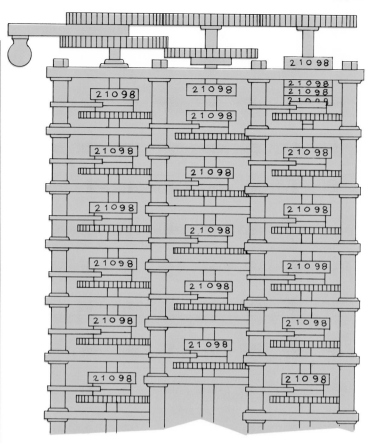

A sketch of Charles ▶
Babbage's design for a
calculator, a type of
computer. As the user fed
in numbers, cogs turned
to the answer.

▲New computers are
designed and tested in
laboratories like this.

When Charles Babbage began
working on his calculating
machine in 1832, little did he
dream what it would lead to.
His idea was right, but he never
finished his project. Over a
century later, in 1945, the first
electronic computer was built
in the United States. In 1947,
the transistor shrank computers
from room size to typewriter size.
Computers now control airport
traffic, road traffic, nuclear power
stations, auto factories, and coal
mines. Today, some computers
can even read!

Tomorrow's Inventor

It isn't likely that a person without a science background will invent things in the future. The days of an amateur inventor, like Thomas Edison, are coming to an end. No longer will inventors work alone on just their own ideas. Today, people working as teams in well-equipped laboratories invent most of our new gadgets and machines. Perhaps computers themselves will some day design other computers, or even become the inventors of the future.

▲ An artist's idea of what a space station in the future may look like.

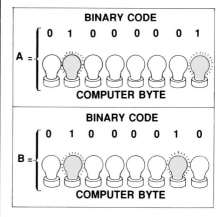

▲ Computers work with on-off switches that represent binary numbers, those made up of 1s and 0s. Shown here are the numbers 65 and 66.

Glossary

Arch: A curved structure, usually built to support weight above an opening, such as a door or a large room. Arches can be built of stone, wood, or metal.

Astronomy: The study of the stars and planets and other bodies in the sky.

Axle: A rod or round bar that holds a wheel so it can turn. A turning, or rotating, axle is fastened to the wheel so that both turn together. A fixed axle stays still while the wheel turns, or revolves, around it.

Babylon: A great capital city in ancient Mesopotamia.

Ballistics: The study of the motion of bodies hurled through the air, such as bullets and cannonballs.

Barometer: An instrument used to measure the pressure of the atmosphere, or air. A barometer can forecast a change in the weather and find the height above sea level, for example, of a mountain.

Battering ram: A war machine used in ancient and medieval times to smash open gaps in the walls or gates of castles or towns.

Block and tackle: One or more pulleys, with rope or cables, used for pulling or lifting large, heavy objects.

Charcoal: A form of carbon made by burning wood or other vegetable or animal substances in little or no air.

Combine (KOM-bine): A harvesting machine that cuts grain, separates the kernels from the husks, and blows the grain into a truck, all in one operation.

Compass card: A card showing the 32 points of the compass — north, south, east, west, north-northeast, northeast, east-northeast, and so on.

Cretans: People who live or lived on Crete, an island in the Mediterranean Sea.

Electrons: Tiny centers of negative electric charge that circle the nucleus of an atom.

Floppy disk: A flexible plastic disk that is placed in a computer. It stores data, files, and programs. Some floppies are enclosed in a rigid plastic cover.

Gas mantle: A lacelike hood placed over a gas jet. It is made of a heat-resistant material that glows white hot in the burning gas flame and gives off light.

Geometry: The branch of mathematics that deals with the measurement, properties, and relationships of points, lines, angles, surfaces, and solids.

Harness: The leather gear of a draft animal — horse, mule, or other animal. It usually is made up of a bridle, reins, blinders, collar, girth, and so on.

Harrow: A device pulled by a horse or tractor, used by a farmer for breaking up and leveling plowed ground to prepare it for seeding. It can be a disk harrow or a spike-tooth harrow.

Hypodermic: A fine, hollow needle for injecting medical drugs into a patient's blood vessel or muscle or under a patient's skin. The term means "under the skin."

Irrigate: To water soil and crops by channeling water from wells or rivers into ditches to irrigate the land.

Keel: The main wooden or metal piece that runs along the entire bottom of a boat or ship and supports the frame.

Laboratory: A room or building where scientific tests, experiments, and other procedures are carried out.

Lever: A bar used to move an object. A seesaw is a simple lever.

Lyre: A harplike stringed musical instrument used by the ancient Egyptians, Greeks, and other ancient peoples.

Macadam: A paving material for road surfaces, made of tiny stones, now usually mixed with tar or asphalt.

Mesopotamia: The land between the Tigris and the Euphrates rivers in what is now Iraq. The rivers run into the Persian Gulf.

Meteorites: Chunks of stone or metal from outer space that strike Earth.

Middle Ages: A period of history from about AD 480 to the late 1400s in Europe. This time of history is also known as the medieval period.

Navigation: A method of finding your way from one place to another. It is a way of finding the position of a ship, airplane, or spacecraft by scientific instruments.

Original: The earliest example of a thing or something entirely new.

Pendulum: A weight that hangs and can swing back and forth freely. Because a pendulum's swings are regular, some types of clocks use pendulums to help them keep time evenly.

Phoenicians: Peoples who lived in about 2000 BC-1000 BC in the eastern Mediterranean lands. They developed navigation, sailing, and trade.

Pig iron: Iron made in blast furnaces, so called because it is often molded in bars known as "pigs."

Pulley: A small wheel that turns inside a case that can be fastened at one or both ends. A rope or chain runs over or under the wheel and is used for lifting loads.

Reaper: A reaping machine used by farmers for harvesting grain. Reapers are used for cutting grain in North America and Australia.

Renaissance: A time in European history between the early 1300s and the late 1500s. At that time, people were greatly interested in art and science and made many discoveries and inventions.

Satellite: Something that circles around a planet, such as the Moon around Earth. Artificial satellites are sent up from Earth.

Semites: A group of peoples who speak Semitic, an early Middle Eastern language group. In ancient times, they included Carthaginians, Assyrians, Hebrews, and Phoenicians.

Sound barrier: A buildup of air pressure as an airplane approaches the speed of sound. When the airplane breaks the sound barrier — speeds past the speed of sound — there is a loud sonic boom.

Spokes: Rods or bars that spread out from the hub of a wheel to its rim. A wheel made with spokes is lighter and stronger than one made from a solid disk.

Sternpost: The main post at the rear of a ship. On many ships, this post supports the rudder.

Stirrup: A metal loop with a flattened base hanging by a strap from each side of a saddle. The rider places a foot in the stirrup to brace his or her body when riding a horse. Stirrups freed the hands of ancient central Asian warriors.

Sumerians: A people who lived in Sumer, Mesopotamia, from about 3500 BC to 2000 BC.

Symbol: A sign, like a letter of the alphabet, that stands for an idea or a sound.

Telegraphy: A way of sending messages over a long distance. The telegraph messages are often made up of Morse code — a system of dots and dashes invented in the 1800s. Originally, telegraphy used wires. Wireless telegraphy, using radio waves, developed later.

Thresher: A piece of farm machinery that separates cut grain from chaff and straw.

Token: A sign, symbol, or mark, often in the form of a coin. Token money has often been used. But it has no value in itself, only what it stands for.

Transistor: A small electronic device used in computers, radios, and TV sets. It controls the flow of electrons like a valve.

Triphammer: A high-speed, power-driven hammer used to shape small articles, such as tool or machine parts.

Vacuum: An empty space. A vacuum bottle, designed for keeping liquids hot or cold, has a vacuum between its glass double walls.

X-ray tube: A special type of vacuum tube made to send out x-rays — waves of a certain kind of electrical and magnetic energy that can go through the human body. You cannot see x-rays. They are used by doctors and dentists to show the inside of the body on film so they can study what is there.

Yarns: Fibers of wool, silk, cotton, flax, or other materials spun into a long strand. Yarns are used in weaving, knitting, crocheting, and similar activities to make various kinds of cloth or fabric garments.

Yoke: A curved piece of wood placed over the necks of draft animals and fastened to a plow or cart that the animals pull along.

Index

A **boldface** number shows that the entry is illustrated on that page. The same page often has text about the entry, too.